Etchings

John Kavanagh

Acknowledgements are due to the following publications, in which some of these poems first appeared: *The Inward Eye, Poetry Ireland Review, The Salmon, Force 10, Aerings* (Leeds), *Flaming Arrows*, RTE Radio 1. A special thanks to Leo Regan for much help and advice.

Cover by Kate McDonagh
Typeset by Nova Print, Galway
Printed by Colour Books, Dublin
Hardcover binding by Kenny's Fine Binding, Galway
Photo by Declan Bray

© John Kavanagh, 1991. All rights reserved.

ISBN 0 948339 74 8 Hardcover £8.50
ISBN 0 948339 75 6 Softcover £4.95

Salmon Publishing, The Bridge Mills, Galway

Contents

Etchings	9
Lamentation	10
At Fort Louis	12
Terms	14
Lines Written on the 75th Anniversary of Gallipoli	15
Incision	17
Night Symphony	18
Celebration	19
Voyagers	20
In Memory of John Laughing Bear (Aged 23 Deceased)	22
At the Hawk's Well Theatre	24
Currach	25
Snapshot	27
Sharing a Train Ride with a Lotus Blossom	28
Sighting	29
Cloudburst	30
Ex-patriots	32
Preparation for a Homecoming	34
Musee d'Historique - Iraklion, Crete	35
New Years Day	37
Mousetrap	39
Prague Spring Morning	40

Leavetaking	41
The Mind of Seasons	42
Aftermath	43
Scream	44
Icarus on Icaria I - IV	45
Dancing with Her Sister	51
Sunday Morning Rain	53
Matin - 3-5-86	54
Visit	55
November	57
Late Saturday Afternoon	58
Apologia	59
The Wooing of Emer	60
Long Distance Love	61
Frog	62
Night Falls	63
Homecoming	64
Meditation on a Morning Train	65
Excavations	66
Sitting	67
Vultures	68
Token	69
Hurdy-Gurdy man	70

For Dermot Collery -
from one who listened ... sometimes

Etchings
For Kate

Standing we looked
upon the table
where you had left them

There were four
- rectangles of black
and white-grey

Moon-shapes and mounds
breastlike
sang to us.

We stooped together and listened.

The prints you finished
in Dublin
left me shaken.

I looked upon you
and wondered.

It was cold and quiet
in the kitchen
the night
you unveiled yourself
to me.

Lamentation
For K.M.

'The baby died, the chord choked it'
was all she managed,
her own strangulated cry
invades me

I hear it again and again
by this grassy edge
of railway track

It stops me

I can go no further
but look anywhere
for anything
to banish sad and desolate cries
of love and grief

across this vast separateness
of mountain and sea

How lovely he might have been
that first born,
love-child of Europe coupling Africa
no gain in mind for once,
but life and love

What hope in each of us
is crushed by this news?

A swift swooping close
startles my feet,
a raw wind ripples the meadows.
I gather myself
and move on.

We must all move on.

At Fort Louis
For K. O'B.

It was the first neap tide
tonguing the shore,
the first slip of an untried prow
on a mirror of water
when you and I embraced

under a canopy of apple and beech,
the black night softening
against a spray of mist,
backlit in a stain of orange light
seeping from the town.

On the gravel path outside the house
limbs adrift like caravels on the high seas
afraid of falling off the edge of a world,
I heeded the semaphore
of your fingers
and mouths like sails unfurled
caught wind.

You berthed in the shelter
of an earlobe,
I dropped anchor in an ocean of cheek
and sensing the pulse of a tremor
searched out an epi-centre.

Its throb vibrating me
from fingertip to knob of wrist
we came ashore,
I in a silver sea-sprayed
charcoal of hair,
you in the warm dark shelter
of a pectoralled valley.

Terms
For K. O'B.

In the opaque lusture
a dull grey of pearl
settled over the skins of her eyes
he sees her resist
better than any walled town
- drawbridge raised
water and provision lain.

He would not storm
crowded battlements
but ring bristling walls
with army and train,
banish camp followers
and settle into patient siege

without recourse
to firebrand or engine of war
that in time she would
raise portcullis and admit
Emissary affection and Ambassador Gift
seeking favourable terms.

Lines Written on the 75th Anniversary of Gallipoli

My grandfather John Patrick Kavanagh
no more than a boy of seventeen, urgent to see the world
joined up and left here as he had wished,
the world at his booted feet, embarking for the Dardanelles
where Connacht skin softened by incessant rains
burnt raw until it wept for butchered friends
in the Gallipoli sun. In three months
he had seen enough to last a lifetime.

Four years later he limped quietly home
unsung like many, better off than most perhaps
dragging a right leg till the day he died.
He never left again - except for that one week
he honeymooned his bride in Dublin,
an indolent countrywoman from Kilmaceown
whose black hair roosted over bog-pool eyes.

I pestered him before he died,
those good-natured ways unfaltering
as the picketlines of cancer gained a foothold,
displaying no sign of pain or the gnawing discomfort
of a creeping bombardment.

Perhaps all that was suffered then,
lying for days in some shellhole right leg ripped to shreds
on Turkish wire, blistered cheeks pressed to scalding sands,
tongue large with thirst awaiting capture or death,
prepared him for such silent dignified end;

Ageing head held up on shrinking shoulders,
that slippered right foot shuffling on linoleum
as he gathered me to the warm smells of brown tweed
to quiet incessant questioning,
a calling halt to the short-trousered pursuit
of irritated cats under table and chair.

He sat me on his knee, high as a king
and there we shared hot sweet tea like soldiers would
from a blue-striped mug big as a bucket,
insides brown as his uniform he said,
tasting noisily off the spoon
before announcing his approval,
then I - copying each measured move and gesture,
his warm hand smoothing the hair from my forehead.

Incision

On a stolen night
we walked by the river's edge
by the crumble and drip
of old walls, shivering
into December,
gloved fingers around each other,
wrapped against a cling of fog
blowing off the water.

Scarf, glove, hats snowed softly
when fingers freed from calf-skin
and lambswool brailled
for cheek and damp hair...

You left me blinded, fumbling
for stolen breath, skin split
to view quickened pulse,
a pink-green of viscera,
the bloodrun on a scalpel tip

That winter night
you sucked gently on my lips
and laid a blade of tongue on mine.

Night Symphony

Sitting at the bed's edge
aching,
sweat running,
an empty bottle of Ouzuo
mocking from a tabletop

I watched them sleeping
curled between sheets
and tip-toed
to steps outside

- sat in a world
of whitewashed walls,
flat-roofed houses
resting under an orange moon

and tuned in to the night symphony
head throbbing
in time to cricketsong
a tap's dripping in the hall

the aged French bodybuilder
muscles veined
and sagging
snoring in his room.
The island dogs duelling in the night.

'God bless the corner of this house
And be the lintel blessed
And bless the hearth and bless the stone
and bless each place of rest'
Verse accompanying a lighted picture
of the Sacred Heart, Inis Mor, Aran.

Celebration

Treading to a cold stone kitchen
shaded from stark light
I search out utensils in unfamiliar places
and sit in a warm Aran dawn.

Above me he watches, enshrined
in his holy frame, eternal. Omniscient.
Beneath a bulb, filamentous, resonant,
streaks glass and stone crimson.
He stares benignly down
all knowing voyeur of guilt.

Through the hallway she sleeps
I watch through half-open doors
listening to the rattle of knife on delft
the trickle of tea

butter sliding onto bread,
breaking it,
crumbs dancing on the tabletop.
Smiling, I remember the catholic love
we made in this quiet house.

Voyagers

The sight of them preserved
yellowed in tall jars
or stretched and pinned
upon dissection boards
reminds me

of April mornings here,
droplet ridden air hangs
light, fresh,
resplendent with damp odours
of Spring

when tumbling as a child
down the garden path
I often stopped
to look upon
random trails of glaze

left behind when they coursed
majestically,
fleets of them, heads high,
horns taut,
sensitive to the touch,
on uncharted voyages
streaming like eels
to the Sargasso.

I would set course
and track them
balled in their shelters
under the hedgerows
to stare at the stilled shells
and sing -

'Snail, snail stick out
your horns
the king is coming
to see you'

and at my chanting of ancient magic
they would emerge
curious, strangely aroused
beginning the bewildered journeys
of the dispossessed

clutching meagre dwellings
to their backs
crossing Oceans of concrete
in unprotested resignation.

In Memory of John Laughing Bear
(Aged 23 Deceased)

In January the Dakotas are empty
spreading to the winds,
and the tourists have gone.
The old man and I
huddled inside the gate

and heard again
the caged crack snap the night in two,
saw him slumped
across an unmade bed
the walls splashed the colour
the beer sign sprays after sundown.

My collar whipped
stinging an ear,
the old man stood still
a drop from his nose
arcing, falling
I followed its damp specking
of the snow

watched grey eyes slip
from flat grey slab
to the burnt sand colour
of the hills,
rivered cheeks blue as steel,
white hair swelling behind.

'Do you miss him'
I asked,
the blue red ends of hands shifted
in his pockets,
his sloping shoulders shuddered in the wind
'I guess I do'
he said
eyes settling
where cloudless blue pressed
against the surging brown
'He was my eldest you know'.

At the Hawk's Well Theatre
For Sydney Bernard Smith

gathered twelve, maybe thirteen
paying
for the privilege
of hearing
a neglected poet

in the lobby
read
standing white bearded
pleased with small attentions
tells us
that true art
lies in concealing life

As a fat woman
behind the desk
answered a phone,
church bells burst through
a glass front

and the pipes of the urinals
behind
pissed shrieking jets
into the quiet

it seemed to me
that true art
lies in concealing the contempt.

Currach

I

Beneath the sill of my window
upturned like the carcass
of a beached whale
the damaged currach rests
suspended on wooden blocks.
Stripped of pitch and canvas
grey, bleached ribs exposed, fractured,
curve into the long spine.

I hear the hiss of its roughness
on the water, oars grating
like stiff joints
and see lithe backs
red-burned, glisten with sweat
and salt water
strain to shouts, groans,
visceral mutterings torn
from flagging sinew.

II

I remember the morning after the race
walking the pool drenched shore,
it lay impaled on a jagged
limestone tooth.
Their drunken pull to celebrate the win
was flaccid, loose, the currach driven hard
then crack!
Like bone splinter.

They laughed and staggered home
through the darkness forgetting...

It sits out there proud, broken,
waiting for them to walk
the twisting path to patch
and tar and curl fresh wood
that it may once again resume
its whisper on the bay.

Snapshot

The balding skullcap
of my knee
gleams
when I sit barelegged
and from its centre
anus pink
a fish eyed mound of scar
leers at me

as if hot wax spilling
had splashed
hardening
to a coloured dome
of plastic.

On cold days
it turns
venous blue
almost the colour
of the Greek sky
the evening of the accident.

Sharing a Train Ride with a Lotus Blossom

Was it her fingers
long, thin, delicate?
Fingers that pluck

twanging two stringed
instruments while kneeling
on silk cushions,

dressed in silk robes
that drew me
to the seat beside her?

Or skin coloured warm
as good tea
stirred yellow-brown?

Or a nose fragile
as porcelain
that I would encircle with my lips?

Or almond eyes
that never stilled,
slanting gently upwards?

I shared a train ride
with a Lotus blossom
she would not look me
in the eye.

Sighting

I remember it in the dry,
dust smells of autumn
in Gormley's hayshed,
sunlight blowing warm
through spaces between the lathes,
in perfect long lines,
hot air coloured brown
with hay dust and seed particle raised
in our playing

then our laughter turned to child squeals,
Wellington booted feet scattering
at our town eyes first glimpse
of a sleeping hedgehog
tumbled from its resting place,
sent skidding
into a ditch and away
with a kick from the old man's boot.

Cloudburst
For Mueni

Taken by surprise
we burst ou
laughing
at the hot
cloudburst above

running
dust puffs exploding
at our feet
to shelter in the overhang
of a building.

My head dipped
skimming splashed lips
along a taut curve
of neck

(Your black skin
warm despite
the shock-cold
of the rain)

brushed copper beads
clicking
dangling from tightly
wound hair

gentle metallic
counterpoint
to the snare symphony
of the rainfall.

My first taste
of you
I savour it yet.

Ex-patriots
(For Grace, Stephen, Gerry and Maria,
Nairobi, January 1988)

Red wine swirls around and over
dry palate, contracting tongue;
wetted lips rebel at the hot smoke taste
when we join them
on the crew cut carpet of lawn
cropped once a week
by Joseph who tends the garden
and trees that spill
from their beds, loping languorous shadows
threatening the rose bushes
which no sooner cast away their petal dresses
than have replaced them
within a week it seems.

Passion, bananas, green hand grenades of mangos
lie shouting to be lifted
by the children who skip each morning
before breakfast
to pick the fruit of night fall
or beat spreading branches with bamboo.

Under the fanned hair of flame trees
I search out
a blood pin prick of Mars,
the shy daffodil of Venus - much higher
than it hangs here,
while Orion stands precariously on its head
and sense behind me
the slow swirl of liquid in the glass,

a head thoughtfully lowered;
I wait, silenced by the sprinkled white
dust brush of Milky Way
for its low drone to reach me

'And how are they all at home...'

Preparation for a Homecoming
For Mueni

There is an outpouring,
a tumbling
damburst of lovegush
soaking into myself
and those about me

but I must control
in crowded places
this pulsing exegesis
channeling outward

stem the flow,
divert currents back inside
to sprinkle dry,
undernourished places
desiccated in our partings
- hollow dimmed socket,
shrivelled tongue...

This fluid winds
coursing
through artery and capillary
searching out
forgotten outbursts of marrow
to tingle toe and fingertip
that lie redundant in your absence.

Musée d'Historique - Iraklion, Crete

A stepped entrance
guarded by drooping palms
that slumber in the heat,
sheltered from the chaos of the main road
that coils to a sky-dipped sea.

Inside, box-brown walls, drab in August,
sunshine smells of polished wood
linger like the bored attendants
watching moodily over the exhibits

dulled remnants of Venice
in a Golden Age
or faded Byzantine frescos.

Upstairs, tidied into a corner
scattered mementoes
of the last war, shell casings
bullets, photographs, a helmet or two
recall savage battles.

But there is a photograph
- a man and his son
visible from the waist up
dressed in dark clothes
rough woven from local wools.

They stand, waiting execution against a wall,
the older frail, weatherbeaten,
the younger - softer, skin pinched hard
onto his jawbones.

Both stare wildly, confused,
pupils large, yet locked into that place
where the eye wanders
as fingers slowly tighten on the trigger.

New Year's Day

No huddling against frost
that winked and smiled
as I hitched, alone on an empty road
in the quiet of a New Year's morning.
No tip-tap of solitary footsteps
ringing on shining asphalt
leading south from Letterkenny...

I feel the dip and swell of hills
head down, running through wood,
passing broken, jagged fingers;
scattered remnants of a season's thinning
standing in eery quiet
like photographs of Ypres
in the Great War

Piercing grey skies
where armies of fat clouds wrestle.
I pound on gravelled paths cold,
fingers curled tight around blue thumbs
throbbing in the iced rains.

They spill over me.
I fight. Resisting savagely,
driving on, snatched breath whooshing,
but they win,
flooding sweet memories
...of a night,
warm-wet couplings...
a favourite shelter no longer visited.

I turn and over the hills
winning with each stride,
teeth clenched against cramped thighs,
or the chilled knife-scrape on lungs
fighting to gather and suck
cold air to take me from this desecrated place
spattered with banished images.

Mousetrap

Hearing the metallic snap
my little sister and I ran
to the mustard coloured door
and opened it.
It was there, a brown, furry-finger,
rope tailed.

We saw it not daring to breathe.
The left ear wriggled like an angry head.
shaking in denial, the pink of its inner ear
shocked me with its fineness,
a flesh as formed as my own.

The dark tail beat on white formica,
a jerking high tension cable
that slowed and stilled as we looked.

And it watched us,
a bulging black eye pointing
and I knew that it blamed me,
its head cleaved and crushed
between wood and copper.

How could I tell it
that it was not my fault?
How could I tell it
that this is the way of the world?

We closed the creaking press
and ran to hide from that accusing stare.

Prague Spring Morning
To the memory of Jan Palach,
died Prague 1969

If he goes into the marketplace
dressed like any other
on any other day,
green parkaed, heavy booted,
breath mushrooming against the cold,
and kneels on a frosted spot
in the centre of town

would you stop your cars
to watch, quiet schoolbound children
as he opens a can to dowse,
shoulders lifting as the shock
trickles down his neck

and if he runs a tongue
across his mouth,
tightens stinging eyes
to find a moment's peace,
before he strikes a match
and burns into the silence

will you march with his name
on your lips
into a spring morning
twenty years from now?

Leavetaking
For Fiona, Feb 1989

There is no way to quiet a frantic heart,
the brush of fingertip or a cooling word
is not enough to still the haunted eye

no love can do enough,
sprinkle raindrop on a bed of coals,
quell a riot of tears breaking you in two

and I must go as I have come,
not knowing in the morning
if the hand that will find mine is one I know.

The Mind of Seasons

Does the mind of winter
need to be so cold
to see a pale sun
nest low in the sky
or hear the drip
of icicles into an opaque morning

Should the mind of spring
be fresh, to sense a swell
of colour in the fields
or the click of spade
on the turned earth

Must the mind of summer
race, to see the fat swans court
and smell the wet burst
of vegetation on a country roadside
slipping under the belly of a car

Will the mind of autumn
rest, on feeling gold and brown
and dryness all around
and the bristling stalk tumble
in the slit, slit of a tractor blade?

Aftermath

Battered squirrels leap
from weeping trunks,
jerk like reprieved men
about the sodden lawns,
arch into an evening
ticking with the renewed conversations
of crickets;

steam rises into wet air
seeded with the warm smell
of love spent when the sky straddled the earth.

Scream

He would walk for days deep into
some hidden valley coated with conifer,
where threads of winter streams quicksilver
down its sides to a gouged floor
and a damp wind shivers
across balding pines.

There he would open wide his mouth
and scorch gaping lungs
until the small birds take flight,
air hissing with the beat of wings,
sap-drained branches bend
long haired grasses flatten
and all is stilled.

Then he would return
stick tapping lightly on the roads
passing the long, drenched lines
that would follow in his footsteps
their bare, mute heads hanging.

Icarus on Icaria

I

I would not listen to them gathered around their fires,
wrapped in night blankets talking
above the crack of dry wood in the flames.
Old men, lazy men, sit and watch the white smoke
arrow into the clear blue, dipped scarlet
around the edges by a bleeding sun cry...

'Come sit with us a while sipping
and it will pass,
listen to the sadness in the wailing
of the young goats bleating past
the open doors of evening
feeding on the scorched thin summer grass.'

I walk barefoot along the sands
heed the bubbling wash,
learn from the sea
of push and pull, turn and return,
like the wave-polished stones that spin
beneath white-foamed feet.

There is silence in the pounding,
stillness in the drench of spray,
refuge from the creak of closing doors,
the dark-flinted eyes of fathers who would push
curious daughters behind them
and mothers gathering sons to billowing skirts.

II

Under the olived hills of Parnassus
bone wheels clicked and spun,
entrails singed,
a bearded oracle proclaimed

'Bring forth that which is inside
and that which is inside will save you.
Deny that which is inside and that
which is inside will destroy'.

Its echo hardened the air,
we touched foreheads to the cooling stone
and slipped away, garments rustling
with the leaves that encircled us.

III

I soared high, straightened legs aching behind,
below gulls glided, rust-headed eagles floundered
in the thin air and left me.
I screeched louder than they
the sun hot on my face,
hair fluttering in the breeze,
ears flooded in blue-white silence

and reaching for the throbbing sun
caught molten beams on splayed palms
glowing like hot coals and I saw all then
- muscle, sinew, bone,
sun, moon, star,
ending and beginning.

I could not stand such sight,
everything transparent,
the crazed, aimless dance of atom,
the sounds of blood tumbling through vein.
The whitehot shock of knowing
hurled me from the skies.

Waters lapped on choking lungs,
I floundered, flapping sodden wings,
hands and feet held fast to wood
and matted feather, half drowned
until the island's boats edged near
and rope-rough hands pulled me from the sea.

IV

With cold blade pressed to my neck
I lay, resistance flown, sobbing for dry land
savouring the press of hard bodies,
their brute tongues chatter on the swell
the lifting scent
of salted cork, the creak of woods

grateful for mercy I had no call for then,
trussed up in old nets, cast onto a beach
for woman, man and child to poke
and light fires around,
for three heat-scalded days and blessed cool nights
dancing their bird-man's fall singing:

'Come sit with us a while sipping
and it will pass,
listen to the sadness in the wailing
of the young goats bleating past
the open doors of evening
feeding on the scorched thin summer grass.'

Tides turned, boats pulled away to plunder the lost
or race to where swirling flocks descend,
screaming onto fresh shoals that wheel past the island,
left me split skinned, swollen tongued
to crawl from the sun
and the sharpened feet of their children

V

Here I live sparingly; gull's eggs, salted fish,
the brined contents of a barrel -
votive offerings from the sea,
sustained by that which would destroy
would I escape this rugged place
or leave the shelter of a stone hut
abandoned in desperation by another.

I pass the village sometimes
nothing's changed
young men lace holed nets, laughing as I pass
threaten any who would push on her dark hair
offering an eye.
The old men's invitations still clatter

across the stone to beckon,
voices sitting somewhere between
the savage violence of a son,
the stolen sympathy of a daughter.
The dogs give chase, pull on my rags
or nip a bony ankle.

VI

I will not sit with them and sip watered wine
and wait for it to pass,
listen to the sadness in the wailing
of the young goats bleating past
the open doors of their evening
feeding on scorched thin summer grass

but watch from far the white smoke's rise,
await anothers plummet from the skies,
trussed up, beaten and kicked half dead
crawl to my soothing herbs and rumpled bed,
to finish what was once begun
for I have flashed an antler at the sun.

Dancing with Her Sister

I've watched them on Saturday nights
dancing, swaying in dimmed light
anonymous,
close, unhurried as oils sliding
on polished glass.

'I feel like a traitor
dancing with you, betraying
my parted lover' he said
'Yet...'

Dancing with her sister
agreed with him,
running fingers along new trails,
smelling new heat, fresh scented,
along a length of spine snake sinewed,
slender hips swivelling in rhythms
he would never match
yet, drawing answers
that had lain uncoaxed.

Dancing with her he sensed
from the tilt and weight of head
pressed onto his neck
that she wanted him too

But they kept their distance
slipping from tentative fingers
tracing whirlpools on a nape,
sloping from skimmed cheeks

'Isn't there hurt enough'
I heard her say
and watched him gently
draw his hand away.

Sunday Morning Rain

Falling, insistent, sliding off
waxed bonnets and chrome bumpers,
stealthily soaking through the rusted wings
of cars parked in Sunday-quiet driveways

clinging to old ladies, Sunday-bests,
mass bound steps,
ringing on drizzled footpaths,
plopping on collapsed bags
from grey slip-by clouds

on to the young crocci and polyanthus'
sliding along stems
of fresh grass
to the wakening earth that opens
its mouth and drinks.

Matin 3-5-86

Passing the burnt out Fire Station
I heard above
the dull throb of a church bell
half human shrieks
of a dog trapped
its screams curdled the morning air

Opposite, travelling people
gathered in the doorways
of dishevelled caravans laughing,
cigarette smoke and voices hanging,
waiting for kettles to boil
and the women to cook breakfast

Their children played barefoot
in the cold,
panting, squatting,
fingers pointing in bemusement.

Visit

I have a photograph
still folded on my desk
both of us standing outside a Navan pub
in watery May light,
my right arm rounding
a fragile waist,
she giddy, straining to get away,
an arm thrown wide in resignation.

She came to visit last friday
for the first time in three years.
I opened the door to darkness
peppered with shaken snow
billowing about the porch.

On sunday, gathered into long coats
wrapped against wavesplash,
ears ringing from the nip in the North wind,
we walked at Raughley
heads freshened by salt smells,
over black volcanic stone where
pushing through like tumours,
white, calcarious weed and coral
entombed once are yielded to the sea.

Squatting by rock pools
covered with cellophane sheets of salt ice
we looked upon tiny sea shrimp darting
through their dark worlds.
I speared membranous coverings with a finger
but quickly pained withdrew it
frozen to my tongue.

Sitting on separate rocks
she chatted calmly,
I clasped a whiplength frond of weed
olive tinged, cast out of the sea,
beating it on rough shale,
its slap and clatter ringing like a metronome
while we waited for the sun to leave,
then turning back,
I hurled my frayed and tattered ropeweed
spinning to the deep.

Later in the hours when an icy grey
mingled with the night
I stirred to her call shivering
in the hallway near her room
where she prepared with delicate sounds;
water splashing, fabrics brushing,
the muted creaking of a door.

Then I waited for the roughness
of engine bark and tyre's bite
standing in the flaring shadows
that burst across the room.

November

Yesterday the yellowed leaves
of cherry blossom
stirred gently
or hung droop-tired

a pair of rooks perched
on the roof
opposite my window
preening themselves
against a thrush egg sky.

Today the sky is still,
flecked with grey
the cherry blossom
a skeletons hand
stripped bone thin
in an icy wind.

The rooks screech upwards
merging with the blue.

Late Saturday Afternoon

Outside through
darkening windows
autumn fingered branches
swayed, dying,
rust coloured leaves
quivered
in winds cooling breath

and the fire still chuckled
in the grate,
its sunburst cackles
shadowing
on the walls

when I awoke
from sudden sleep
which poured
sliding
a hot lava'd balm
rolling
in to the corner
of an eye
melting one lid to another.

Apologia

I read your note
and hear the voice
of one lost
crying in the wilderness

and see your eyes
rounded as ripened fruit
dripping in to me.

The Wooing of Emer

*'Cuchulainn himself went to a place
called the gardens of Lug to woo
a girl he knew there. Her name was Emer.'
- The Táin, trans, T. Kinsella*

I am coolness of mountain streams
rushing to the Ocean's lips
that would swallow me

I am sunlight
scattering beams into the dark,
whispering dust into a dance

I am the silvered salmon
leaping at the white moon
hanging over a black stillness of lake

I am the swallow flying south
thawing frosted wings,
offering sweet song to the trees

I am the wounded stag
bellowing bloodied victories
through hooded valleys

I am green seed
fingering the warm earth
that I might suck.

Long Distance Love
For Mueni

We must bend
time
but also space
curling
compacting each
into the other

into each other

into journeys
too infrequent
between
dull
dark longings.

Frog
for Seamus Heaney

Squatting under damp cuttings
a fat greeness
chest swelling and shrinking
to a secret frog pulse.

I did not know how long
it had been there under
the criss-crossed stumps of the wood pile
perhaps a day or more

since dog first sniffed cautiously
at the frantic enmeshed leaping
banging off damp wood.
Reaching between lengths

of twisted stick I gripped
cold blooded fullness
coated with coal and wood dust
lifted firmly, threw high

beyond the concrete wall
into the wet field
listening
to a silent toss limbed shout of joy.

Night Falls

A forefinger blackens from root to tip
enveloped in the cold skin
of the night
when I point to silver salted skies,

to the winking headland
that floats on the coal-coolness of sea,
or skim along
all that is familiar,
ditch, fence, bramble patch,
scattered, solitary trees
melting into a sooted curtain
of darkness.

Homecoming
For Mueni

A mouth nestles close
its globe-cheeked windsacks,
fill and empty in sleep's rhythms;

lips purse,
narrow as a hollow nippled bellows tip,
whisper warm air
sweet as Pineapple
down unlit tunnel of ear.

Her spoon fingers stir
in the tangled rain forests
of my hair.

Meditation on a Morning Train

Behind us
dawn undresses

the bride-shy sun
peeps

into a sky
of Berber blue

brightening
frost-breathed fields.

Thoughts come
and go

some float
light as a leaf-twirl

some crash
down

heavy
as a boulder's fall.

Excavations

Pins, sandals, seeds burnt black
- excavated artefacts,
stumbled on inadvertently like unknown dents
in familiar landscapes
or the chink of spade ringing
off something new

the parting of topsoil, cleaving through
green shoots, tendrils
white, light-shy,
breaking crusted, clinging earth

bowing with trowel and horsehair
to ease out from dark tombs
where they had lain hidden,
chalices of burnished gold

brushing clay from shattered bones
that sit in trays, orange-damp,
ready for washing,
twisting stringed tags
to catalogue with others.

Such are memories.

Sitting
For Kate

You look at me then away again
eyes darting like one trapped.

In time I have come
to know you better than any.

Who else has seen the hints
and cracks of crows feet

when your eyes tighten in a smile
or furrows ploughed in concentration?

The scraping passes unnoticed,
eyes lock, searching

I move again. You chastise.
I rearrange my attentions

a restless model
uneasy with your gift.

Getting to know the sounds
on black cardboard

of your crayon spreading me
I watch you

listening to the distance
that has come between us.

'...it was, he said, the greatest tragedy
he had encountered in his time as Coroner.
He was critical of the 'gutter press'
coverage of the incident, saying that this
had only added to the terrible suffering
of the families involved.'
- 'Sligo Champion'
Friday, Sept. 16th 1988, report on
the inquest on the death of student
nurse Sarah Tarpey and Cathal McManus.

Vultures

What does it matter how
but that he was disturbed enough
to cut and file and smuggle
in a bag

- that she lay in the corridor
where he called her,
Sternum split by the blast
from a sawn-off
and the walls running with blood;

that he ran quickly
to a closet, pushing both barrels
under his chin
and squeezed again?

Is all of this not enough
to halt the tabloid hacks
who would harass her classmates
looking for the stained sheets
of a relationship
and lie their way into his rented room?

Token

Running a warm palm along
cool hardness
I picked it up and opened it.
The spine crackled noisily
clustered pages reluctantly separating,
the crisp, white, starch-stiffness
clumped tightly as a fist.

Before wrapping it badly
in brown paper
I scratched a line or two…

Now, on infrequent visits
I sometimes ease it
from where it stands
pressed between others
that threaten in their corpulence
to overwhelm it
(bursting the light rosewood casings)

And placing it on the table
speculate its ageing leafends
stained sand-brown,
some dogeared, some underlined
with care.

Stiffness smoothed from that long back
it rests, pages flipping easily,
spreading itself to any
who would take time to pluck it
from the shelf of anonymity.

Hurdy - Gurdy Man
For Donovan

Fortyish now, tousled, boyish yet,
you arrived armed to the teeth
with a smile and the machinery to kill fascists
- harmonica strapped about your neck and that old, old guitar
still embellished with its wizard's half moon
soundhole and yellow stars.

The voice startles, better perhaps than ever,
a youth-gentle vibrato
that trembles, lingers under roving eyes
that twinkle along two hundred of us
as you talk of the Beatles, Mia Farrow,
a Beach Boy and yourself at the Maharishi's ashram.

It's a long way now it seems, from those nights
under tropical Indian stars
and the packed houses of Madison Square Garden
to a half-filled room in the Silver Swan
on a Thursday night,
the air lightly scented with banned substances
that you were so fond of once.

Sitting up there buddha-calm yourself,
smiling, you seem happy to be back.